UNSCATHED

UNSCATHED

AMARA UGO EZE

TEMPLATE BOOKS®

UNSCATHED

Amara Ugo Eze
Copyright © 2019
All rights reserved
ISBN: 978-978-976-479-2

Published in Nigeria by
TEMPLATE BOOKS®
(+234)8053506113, 7062027312
info@templatebooks.com, templatebooks@yahoo.com
www.templatebooks.com

All scripture quotations are from the King James Version & New King James Version of the Bible, except otherwise stated.

To God, My Everything;
To My Ever Supportive
Husband and Best Friend,
To My Adorables:
Chibuikem and Kenenna,

To my very special Mother,
THANK YOU

ACKNOWLEDGEMENT

I want to specially thank a man whose deep insights in the word of God taught me how to practically fight the fight of faith and obtain my inheritance in Christ, Pastor Poju Oyemade. Thank you so much Sir, for always dividing the word of truth rightly. I and my family are ever grateful to you.

Thank you Pastor Matthew Ashimolowo for your passion for God and His people, I keep thanking God everyday for speaking through you on that fateful day. We are grateful Sir.

Thank you Rev Mark Harkins for helping us understand how easy to know who we are in Christ and to always live a life full of joy. Your HolyGhost Meetings are electrifying. Thank you Sir for teaching us how to laugh in the Holy Ghost. We are grateful.

Special thanks to Pastor Nathaniel Bassey. Your Music Ministry has healed so many wounds and reconnected many to Christ. Thank you for yielding to this call. I appreciate you Sir.

To Dr. Linda Ikeji, thank you so much ma for your noble act of sharing my story to the world with your platform. This really inspired my confidence to write this book. I appreciate you ma.

To my brother in law and his amiable wife, Pastor & Mrs Akachukwu Jasper Eze, thank you for your undiluted love and support all through the waiting period. We love you.

To my ever loving siblings, Mrs Chinomso Goodluck, Mr Chukwudi Ajuonu, Dr Chinenye Ajuonu, Mr Emmanuel Ajuonu and Engr Victor Ajuonu. Thank you.

Table of Contents

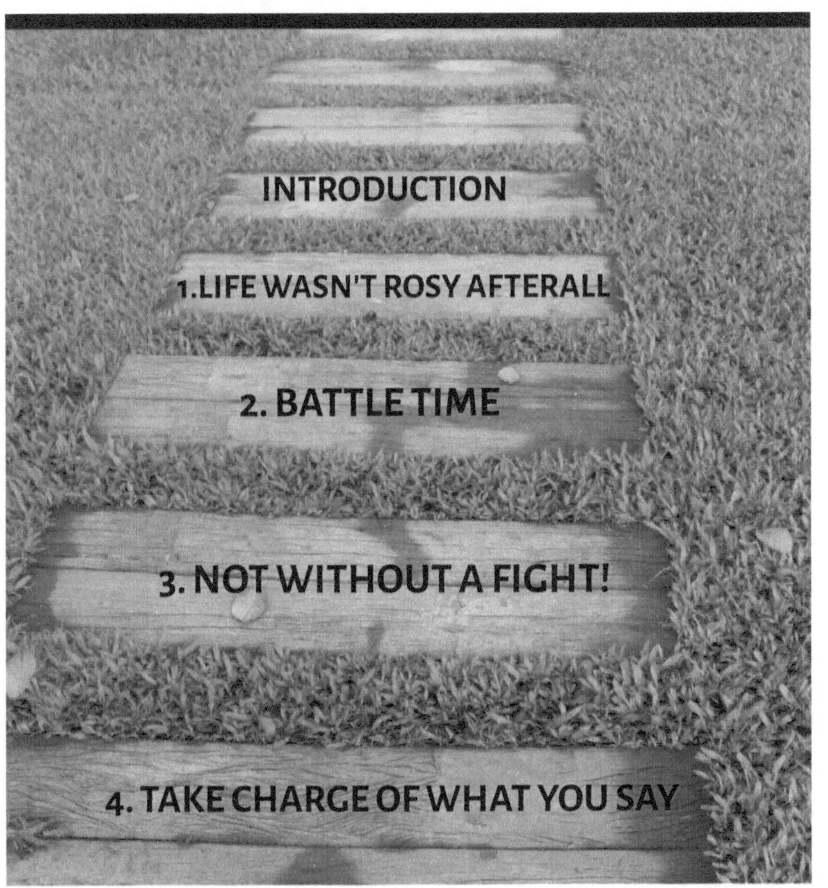

INTRODUCTION

Walking through the journey called life...

Thought it would be all rosy

The thorns didn't let it be cozy

I wanted to handle it with my will

Didn't know I was putting myself in the mill

My heart was almost torn into shreds

The place, so full of uncertainty and dread

I was almost giving up

Until God's hand pulled me up

Walking through the journey called life...

UNSCATHED!!!

CHAPTER ONE
Life wasn't rosy afterall

In a serene and beautiful environment with a very beautiful weather, I said "I do" to the man of my dreams, in the presence of a group of witnesses.

It was an amazing day and we were so excited that we were finally married. We couldn't wait to see what the future had for us. This next stage of our lives meant so much to us and we were grateful to God that the wedding was a successful one.

Finally!!! I could now run from the never ending house chores in my maiden home, I can now live peacefully and stay in charge of my own house! Phew!!! It was a huge relief, little did I know that, just like I ran to my own house, there were also serious responsibilities that were attached to it too to keep the home running smoothly which I couldn't run away from other than to face them headlong. I thought it was going to be a walk in the park, life taught me otherwise...

We settled in nicely and started living our lives as man and wife. I was and am still grateful to God for the man He gave me, a man who loves God with all of His heart. We would pray together, study together, eat together, we literally did everything together. Those early days were indeed so beautiful we were both full and content. One month after wedding, the expected happened! We were pregnant! Oh my God, I was ecstatic and so joyful. I was like, 'so little me could also get pregnant with no hitches', I was just in cloud 9. It was beautiful.

At exactly 8 weeks of pregnancy, I started spotting. As a first time mum I was confused and didn't know what to do but deep within me I felt that something wasn't right. I ran to google and I was told that spotting was normal but when the bleeding increases with cramps then something was definitely wrong that it might lead to a miscarriage.

I was filled with fear, nothing or no one prepared me for this. I had no scriptures to counter these fearful thoughts. I spotted for some days and as the days went by, the spotting was increasing.

I was filled with fear, nothing or no one prepared me for this. I had no scriptures to counter these fearful thoughts. I spotted for some days and as the days went by, the spotting was increasing.

Then on this particular night I started bleeding heavily with serious cramps I didn't know that I was contracting. I cried out in pain, oh it was so painful to watch your baby go without doing anything to save the child. My husband tried his best to console me but the pain was too much to bear. The next day, the doctor inserted a drug and told me that it will help bring out the remnants of the foetus if there was any. Oh the contractions that came with it can't be imagined. It was so so painful but it helped bring out some things.

I went for a scan, and nothing was seen in my womb. So indeed I had miscarried, how I cried my heart out, I grieved the miscarriage like I was grieving the death of a loved one. It was just too painful to bear. I thought it will be all rosy but life threw a hard one at me. That was the first blow, it really took a while for me to heal and move on...

In October that same year, we already moved on and life has gone back to normal. Then I missed my period and went for a pregnancy test and it was positive.

We were excited and started making plans for the baby. My husband pampered me a lot and

I was on top of the moon, I felt so loved and cared for by my family and close friends. Then something happened...At exactly 12 weeks (3 months of pregnancy) I started spotting! Oh my God! Not again!!! My worst fear has come upon me and I didn't still have an idea of what to do to prevent this from getting to the stage of miscarriage. I panicked real good.

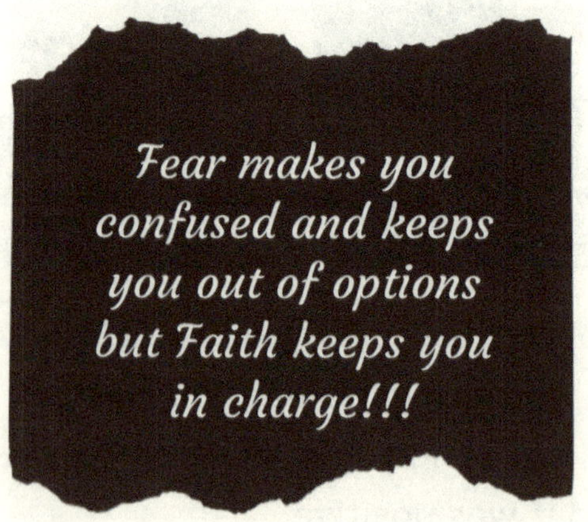

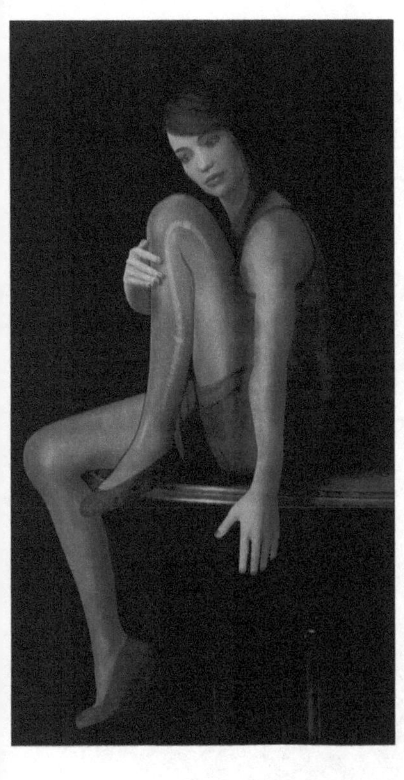

The doctor asked me to stay on bed rest, while at it, lots of horrible thoughts started flooding my mind and I gave heed to them. At the end of the day I lost my baby for the second time. I went through the first process of evacuating the remnants but scan said there were still somethings found, so I was booked for a D&C. I thought the drug insertion process was painful, the D&C was more terrible! The pains can't just be explained. Oh how I wept!

The next day, I made up my mind to weep no more but to remain strong so that I can be able to move on fast. I took myself to a beauty shop and got myself a little bit pampered. Then I went shopping and bought very lovely clothes for myself. I asked the Holy Spirit for strength and He stepped in immediately. Peace engulfed my heart for the first time in a while... The Holy Spirit started speaking to me that this was a battle which I must fight and come out victorious.

For we wrestle not against flesh and blood, but against principalities, against powers, against the rulers of the darkness of this world, against spiritual wickedness in high places…(Ephesians 6:12 KJV). He reminded me that the devil wasn't happy that I'm happily married to a man that loves God and that since the devil knows that we will produce godly seed(Malachi 2:15), he decided to strike us with multiple miscarriages. He told me that I am a joyful mother of godly kids(Psalms113:9) but my faith must be built, nobody can fight this battle for me.

CHAPTER TWO
Battle Time

It was battle time, now I knew who was really behind all my pain and suffering. But I needed to be well prepared for this battle. It took one full year to prepare by studying God's word on what He has said concerning fruitfulness, I listened to Christian tapes on faith, I read faith based books on fruitfulness. I prayed and confessed God's word over my womb and body generally.

I filled my mind with scriptures, thank God for the HolySpirit, He just kept giving me scriptures upon scriptures I never knew existed but were addressing my situation directly. I came into a place of peace, I could literally hear instructions from the Holy Spirit. On one occasion, the Holy Spirit told me to walk into a baby shop and purchase two baby clothes for my children. I obeyed and walked in, not having an idea of what size to buy. I just blurted out that I needed baby clothes they asked, 'What size?' I couldn't speak. The attendant in charge kind of understood my dilemma and decided to help me by showing me some of what they had. I told her to just give me two of the first sets of clothes she showed me.

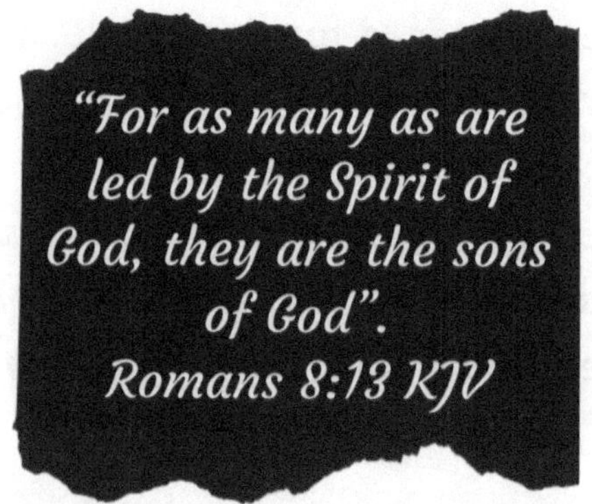

I paid for them and went home. The HolySpirit asked me to bring them out and hold it like I was holding a baby and dance around my room. I danced with all of my heart with an unspeakable joy. The rest of the year passed by without much ado...I still kept up with my daily routine of studying, praying, declaring, praising, dancing God's word over my life. My faith grew tremendously, even though I haven't physically seen my children yet, I knew without a shadow of doubt that I already had them so I was so at peace. By December I wrote this confession from the scriptures I had been studying since that year:

"Confession for the fruit of the Womb I am rejoicing and I'm singing songs of praise to my God because He has made the destinies of my children greater than that of my peers.
He as made me a happy mother of Godly children. My children are like olive shoots round our table and I am like a fruitful vine within my house.
I have the capacity to conceive and carry to full term
With no form of sickness and deliver of my offsprings.
I neither have the capacity to miscarry nor be barren.
The number of our days is being fulfilled by God.
For the Lord has sworn by himself that as surely as He lives I shall wear my children like ornaments, I shall put them on as a bride. He has given me double for every trouble double for every shame. As my children keep coming to me, I shall look and be radiant, my heart will throb and swell with joy I am saying with Elizabeth, 'The Lord has done this for me; In these days He has shown me favour and taken away disgrace among the people'. For ALL things are working together for my good because I love God and am called according to His purpose.
Amen"

This confession of faith became my daily routine, I confessed it day and night. January of the following year came and we were having our annual Faith Believers Conference (WAFBEC) that month. In preparation for it, we embarked on a 21 day praying and fasting. There was a little twist to that year's fast. We were asked to break our fast with food on the first two days, fruits and vegetables on the 3rd day then water on the last day. We were to continue this cycle till the end of 21 days. I and my husband was so determined to do this, so we did. Boy was that easy? No! But we knew we were in a battle and we must come out victorious! On one of the days we were fasting, as I was dancing and praising God, I felt a movement in my stomach I laughed out loud and said 'Thank You Jesus! Its done!!!' I knew in my spirit that we were pregnant. Flesh and blood didn't reveal these words to me, I tell you.

WAFBEC kicked off shortly after the fast, and I have long forgotten the experience I had during the fast. I and my husband just wanted a beautiful experience in His presence. So we just worshipped Him with all of our hearts. In one of the worship sessions with Pastor Nathaniel Bassey, I had an experience that I will never forget in my life... Jesus appeared to me! It was just so glorious!!! He asked me to open my mouth and stick out my tongue, It felt like someone was cleaning out dirt from my tongue. Afterwards, He asked me to place my hands on my stomach and begin to prophesy to my child. He told me that whatever I say over my child's life this time will come to pass cos my tongue has been anointed.

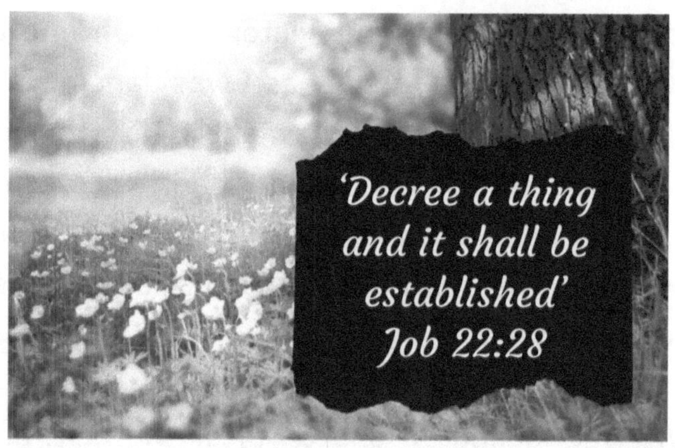

In my mind I was like REALLY??? So a child is in my womb??? I immediately started speaking prophetically to my baby. Oh it was just too glorious! His Presence...I knelt down and wept and worshipped Him. As soon as that encounter ended, Pastor Nathaniel Bassey said, "Jesus is here, already ministering to some people". Now that was my confirmation! I wept some more... It was just so glorious...

The following days of the conference flew by quickly. We were asked in one of the sessions not to take offence in what might happen to us in our personal space, no matter what happens. This is to enable the blessing of God that has already been activated in our lives not to be aborted. I took these words seriously, as I got home, I started having cramps. I was almost getting demoralized, then I remembered those words I sprung up, danced and praised to my heart's content. I got a sanitary pad to use, then I laid down to rest. While I waited for the evening session. The evening came and it was a HolyGhost service by Rev Mark Hankins, oh how we laughed and danced in the Holy

Ghost that night. It was just too powerful! We went back home and I went for my night bath. I checked myself , behold there was no blood. In an instant I knew that it was implantation bleeding that I had earlier.

That was the reason for the cramps. I ran out of the bathroom and shared the goodnews with my husband. We were so joyful and blessed the Lord earnestly for this baby. Knowing fully well that our baby has come to stay...
At exactly 8 weeks of pregnancy I started spotting again cos I travelled to the east to visit my friend. That night I laughed so hard at the devil, my friend had to join me in the laughter. The spotting stopped before dawn the next day. So I came back to Lagos. Things were moving on smoothly until the 12th week...
I started spotting again! This time around I spotted for 7 days! Meanwhile, we kept decreeing and declaring that we do not cast our young before its time and the number of our days God has fulfilled (Exodus). On the 7th day, the spotting stopped, Glory to God! I went for scan and our baby's heartbeat was beating strong, he was growing healthily. I carried on

with the pregnancy till 39 weeks and a day…

At exactly 4am, 25th September 2015, my water broke and mild contractions started almost immediately. By 6am, we got to the hospital and I was just 4cm dilated. They gave me bed and told me I still had a long way to go. I just kept speaking God's word over me and my baby. The nurses kept saying I looked so calm even though this was my first baby. I just laughed and said everything is in control. When I was 7cm dilated, I was rolled to the theater the nurses and doctor in charge left me there. The contractions got more intense and frequent. It got to a point I couldn't hold it anymore I told my husband that I would push the baby out right now. Immediately the doctor came into the theatre and checked me , he felt my baby's head…

With the second push our baby Chibuikem Joshua Eze came forth at exactly 2.30pm. It was a very emotional one for me.

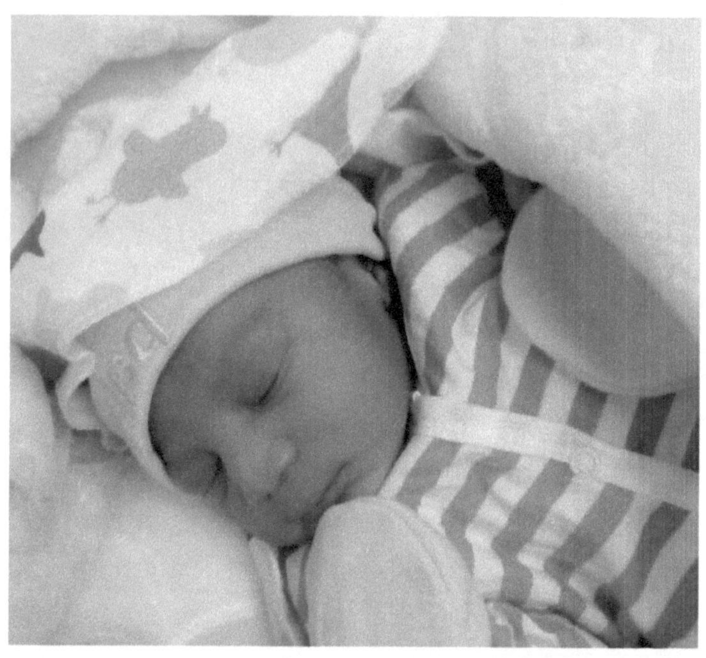

Chibuikem Joshua Eze at birth

As they held out my baby for me, I kept telling myself, "So I'm finally a mother". God indeed is a great God. None of His words returns to Him void until it accomplishes what He has sent it to do. We gave God Glory and thanks for making us joyful parents. Our hearts were full.

CHAPTER THREE

Not without a fight!

"When you pass through the waters, I will be with you
When you pass through the rivers,
they will not sweep over you.
When you walk through the fire,
you will not be burned;
the flames will not set you ablaze".

Isaiah 43:2 NIV

14 Days Postpartum...

Doctor: Is he on admission?

Us: No

Silence...

Reading the doctor's report, amongst other things, we saw..."The child has two holes in the heart..." My legs couldn't carry me anymore, unusual sweat broke out on my forehead, I needed a seat. Someone should please wake me up from this nightmare.. I managed to put myself together and we left the doctor's office. Suddenly, scriptures started flooding my heart and I was strengthened. I held my son up and said, "The sickness is not unto death but to show forth the glory of God".

Earlier that week...

We were still basking in the euphoria of being new parents of a very beautiful baby. Then one fateful morning as I was nursing him, I noticed that he had noisy breathing. I was like well, it could be that he has caught the flu as he was barely 2weeks on earth. I called my husband to see what I heard, he said we should go see a pediatrician. That was how the journey to Chibuikem's diagnosis, hospital trips and the next level of our faith started...

We met with the Pediatrician, she and her team prescribed lots of tests and did some checkups on my baby and all that. My 14 day old baby had to undergo lots of procedures and tests, I too had to carry my tired body to walk through the paths of that hospital, seeking solution. We were such in a very pathetic state... on our way home, we kept speaking God's word over our child and had a very good laugh at the devil

The following morning, I woke up with these words so strong in my heart, 'I will give you a new heart' I immediately searched the scriptures and found it in Ezekiel 36:26.

> "I will give you a new heart and put a new spirit in you; I will remove from you your heart of stone and give you a heart of flesh"
> Ezekiel 36:26 NIV

Now this was a word directly from God to me, I knew it! I knew my son was already healed, I was so joyful! That word in Ezekiel 36:26 amongst other prophetic words became my daily declaration. I spoke it over our son day and night. The drugs the doctors gave us, I discarded them cos they were making my baby cough. It was an intense moment of prayer, studying the word, praise and worship and declaration of our faith for us. We remembered that the doctor asked us when we'll be ready to go to India for surgery and we told her after the second echo scan, we would make a decision. Oh how we prayed!

It was time for our annual Faith Believers' Conference and we had just one prayer point that on the second echo scan Chibuikem Joshua Eze's heart has been completely covered up. We prayed that God will place it in the heart of one of the ministers to prophetically declare it. In one of the evening sessions with Pastor Matthew Ashimolowo, He said it! Yes!!! He did!!! I and hubby was watching online, we jumped up and screamed out loud with joy. We knew like we knew our names that the battle has been won. We have emerged victorious! Our son has been healed!!! Hallelujah!!!! Our joy is full!!!

It was days to the second echo scan, the Holy Spirit instructed me to go on a phone break for 3days. During those 3 days, my phone would be put off and I will praise God all through those days. The last day was meant to be the day for the second echo scan. I obeyed and it was just glorious, it was affirmed all over again that our son has been healed and the world will glorify the name of the Lord with his testimony.

On Friday, we set out to the hospital excited because we already knew what the result will be. The pediatric cardiologist did the scan and was just smiling all through. She told us that the two big holes has been completely closed and there was no need to worry anymore (little did she know we weren't worried at all). Oh I wanted to scream over the roof tops and declare that our God is good! It was a joyous moment for us, we went home and praised our hearts out. God is just too faithful to fail.

It felt so good to know that our son has been completely healed. We remembered the days our son was rapidly loosing weight cos of the condition and would jerk continuously, struggling to breathe and suck breast milk at the same time and we couldn't do anything about it. We remembered the day he was diagnosed and how we reacted to it.

Oh we remembered those trying times and we couldn't help but break down with song of thanksgiving and tears of joy. God's love for us is just too unfathomable, who are we that He is so mindful of us? Chibuikem Joshua Eze is God's perfect gift to us and God made sure He made him perfect for us. We couldn't just contain our joy. We told everyone and anyone who cared to listen. Then I put it up on my Facebook page it got lots of shares, a major blog in Nigeria carried it and boom it went viral. You can check out the testimony by clicking this site: https://www.lindaikejisblog.com/2016/03/lady-testifies-how-god-healed-her-baby.html

I had so many messages and phone calls that week, of people telling me how inspired they were, I also met people that were in same situation as me and how their faith has been strengthened after hearing our testimony. Oh my God! We were overwhelmed, but the most fulfilling part was seeing that God's name was being glorified globally. Oh our hearts were full!!!

CHAPTER FOUR

Take charge of what you say

We became dotting parents to our son, God presented him to us perfectly healed and complete. So it's our duty to furnish him with all he needs and also train him in the way of the Lord. Today, he is growing into a fine young man and we will always be grateful to God for that experience.

2 ½ Years Later...

I found out I was pregnant, I had mixed feelings cos I was about to step into the career world, having lost some years. I wasn't so happy with the new development and started complaining a lot, I forgot so easily how God came through for me in the past. Was like a little child screaming for candy having had an extracted tooth in the past cos of this same candy. I didn't want to think through the consequences of being ungrateful. I kept whining and complaining about the pregnancy pains and discomfort on my hip bone (Symphysis Pubis Diastasis SPD) its common in pregnancy. The more I spoke negatively, the more painful the pains became. When I started getting closer to my EDD, fear came. It was as if the spirit of fear came upon me. I told my husband and he began praying for me. I had to ask for mercy and gradually picked up my prayer life.

I started reading books on faith and resumed my confession. Thank God for His mercy that is always new every morning.

At 38weeks, I went for scan, while I was waiting for the scan I had a nudge to do a write up on fear and share it on my social media handles which I obeyed. As I stepped out of the diagnostic center to set out on my journey home, I had an accident that almost claimed my life and that of my baby. I was brought to the hospital and my doctor monitored my baby all night. To the God's Glory my baby was unharmed. The next day at 9.45am Kenenna Jeddy Eze, my second son, was pulled out to the Glory of God. From my experience I came to realize that often times we don't know when we work in sync with the devil with our words. We think when we say these negative word in other to get attention from others or to get them to empathize with us, we tend to feel better.

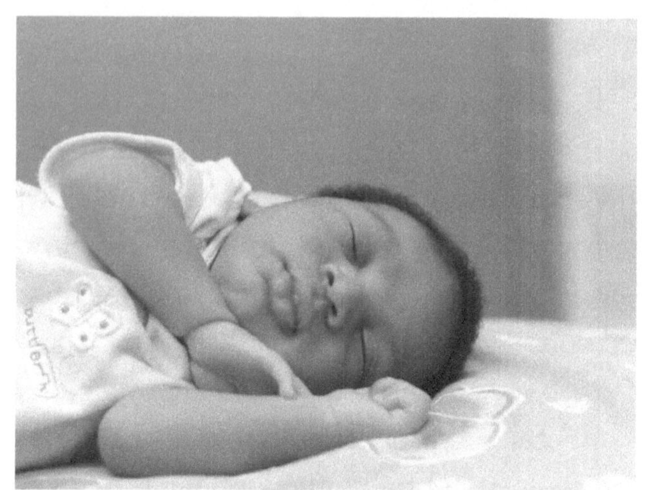

Meet Kenenna Jeddy Eze few days
after birth

My quiver is full. He has made me a
joyful mother of Godly kids

But then we end up empowering the enemy with these negative words. When we walk by faith, we don't look at how we feel. What we look at is what God has said concerning us. Let's not be deceived, the devil goes about like a roaring lion, looking for who to devour. He is not at all our friend and doesn't intend to be. We are what we say in the spirit realm. Always counter that negative thought the devil brings to your mind with the word of God. Remember, as a man thinketh in his heart, so is he.

Notice the pattern, the enemy tries to get you to a stage when you are numb spiritually, He wants you to get to that place of unbelief. Then he inflicts fear in you before giving you a blow. Please don't indulge him. Fear and unbelief has messed a lot of believers up and made them loose what is rightfully theirs.

Always put on the full armor of God that you may be able to withstand the wiles of the devil- Ephesians 6:11. Be tenacious till the end so that you can take what rightfully belongs to you. The devil only comes to kill, steal and destroy. But Jesus came to give us life and life in

abundance. Surround yourself with believers of the same faith who will always uphold you in prayers and never forget the fellowship of the brethren.

Finally my brethren, troubles come so that we can learn to fully trust in God. My pastor will always say, "Never let a crisis go to waste" this is so true. When we are faced with an issue, that's not the time to start throwing pity party. It's the time to get to work and emerge victorious, trusting God all through and learning all you can learn in the process.

In conclusion, remain

undeterred in the face of that trial and tribulation. Let your faith and focus remain solely on God and you'll emerge victoriously unscathed.

I believe my story has helped ignite that unwavering faith in God. God makes all things beautiful in its time. His word never returns to Him void until it has accomplishes what He has sent it to do. Remain steadfast, hold fast your confession of faith. Do not back down, then you'll get into your place of rest and rejoice through it all. I love you all.

If you would like to contact me for speaking engagements,one on one counselling and prayers, please send a mail to amaraugoeze@gmail.com or visit my website by clicking @ www.amaraugoeze.com

You can also reach me via facebook, instagram and twitter @amaraugoeze

About the author

Amara Ugo Eze is a Business Lawyer, an Entrepreneur, a Public Speaker and a writer who loves to teach, empower and inspire others to be the best they can be by living purposefully. She sits as a trustee with an NGO, Empowered Sapiens Mulier Initiative (ESMI) whose major purpose is to empower women with wisdom. She also vounteers as facilitator on legal matters with Beauty in black foundation, an NGO, that promotes and inspires beauty through the use of natural organic products for the preservation of the African skin. She is married with two adorable kids.

TEMPLATE
www.templatebooks.com